Quiet Water

The
Inspirational Poetry
Of
James Kavanaugh

BOOKS BY JAMES KAVANAUGH

NON-FICTION

There's Two Of You
Man In Search of God
Journal of Renewal
A Modern Priest Looks At His Outdated Church
The Struggle of the Unbeliever (Limited Edition)
The Birth of God
Between Man And Woman(co-authored)
Search: A Guide For Those Who Dare Ask Of Life
       Everything Good And Beautiful

POETRY

There Are Men Too Gentle To Live Among Wolves
Will You Be My Friend?
America: A Ballad
The Crooked Angel (a children's book)
Sunshine Days And Foggy Nights
Maybe If I Loved You More
Winter Has Lasted Too Long
Walk Easy On The Earth
Laughing Down Lonely Canyons
Today I Wondered About Love
     (Adapted from: Faces In The City)
From Loneliness To Love
Tears and Laughter Of A Man's Soul
Mystic Fire: The Love Poetry Of
      James Kavanaugh
Quiet Water: The Inspirational Poetry of
      James Kavanaugh

FICTION

A Coward For Them All
The Celibates

ALLEGORY

Celebrate The Sun: A Love Story
A Village Called Harmony - A Fable

Quiet Water

The
Inspirational Poetry
Of
James Kavanaugh

Design And Selections
By Cheryl Pecaut

STEVEN J. NASH PUBLISHING
P. O. Box 2115
Highland Park, Illinois

Cover Photo by Doris Hayes

Kavanaugh, James
    Quiet Water: The Inspirational Poetry of James Kavanaugh
            1. Title

Library of Congress Catalogue # 01-090575
ISBN # 1-878995-20-0

First Trade Paper Edition
Steven J. Nash Publishing

---

10 9 8 7 6 5 4

ACKNOWLEDGMENTS

My gratitude to Cheryl Pecaut
and Carleton Whitehead.

DEDICATION

To those who taught me of the quiet water within.

Especially
To those who refuse to live without peace and
passion, joy and laughter.

INTRODUCTION

For centuries philosophers and theologians have struggled to define man's relationship with God. While some asked the universe for answers, others were said to have received a private revelation from above. Each leader attracted devout followers, many of whom insisted that their way was the only way, as if God were an elitist condemning all but the elect. In the name of this same God, innocent blood was shed and unbelievers were often condemned to a lifetime of rejection and an eternity of pain.

Gradually, wise and gentle teachers questioned a God Who would arbitrarily condemn any of the special creatures who were granted dominion of the earth. Why would a loving God Who gave the gift of life not make Himself accessible to all alike -- even without the intercessory power of celebrated high priests or prophets? How could He reject those who never heard the evangelists who claimed to be His exclusive messengers? It appeared that men and women of every sect and creed, even those who sincerely questioned God's existence or denied it, lived good and loving lives beyond reproach.

With time's passage and the expansion of research and communication, it became clear that each culture, east or west, had developed its own system of contact with this Higher Power. The cults and creeds, oracles and apparitions, statues and totems seemed far more similar than divergent. It was as if each color and climate of men devised its own simple or elaborate laws and rituals to span the gulf between heaven and earth. And in every land as well, there were those who privately or publicly questioned the orthodox dogmas and mores that governed the masses.

Even the most ancient and powerful of the sects were challenged, as the heretics of one generation became the heroes and leaders of the next. What began in bloodshed and banishment was almost suddenly evolving into broader understanding and universal brotherhood. This is not to ignore the vendettas from the past still made sacred in the present, but to recognize that growing numbers of men and women were discovering a Divinity within themselves. Their God by whatever name or definition, or without it, guided the lives of His children with the same loving energy that nourished trees and animals and kept intact the universe.

It did not matter whether men called Him by name or honestly ignored Him. He was not the God of a single race or a unique and narrow revelation. He was the God of every emperor and starving child, of great minds and the retarded, of laughing children and lonely old men, of ones in vibrant health and others genetically scarred from birth. Those writhing in agonizing pain or lacerated by sudden tragedy might curse His name and desecrate His concern. Those lulled in luxury or lost in power and success might mock His omnipotence and ridicule His laws. No matter. He is the unconditional lover, as available to those who scorn Him as to the prayerful and devoted. He leads and guides and cherishes whether I laud His mercy or never give Him a thought.

Prayer and fasting, incense and sacrifice are not essential conditions of His love. He is immediately available to everyone at any time or in any place, because His altar and energy rest in the hearts and minds, in the very cells of all His children. For years I adored Him in ritual and habit, and then ignored Him in anger and silence. I was baptized in guilt, confirmed in sadness, and ordained in fear, then
"fled Him down the nights and down the days and
down the labyrinthine ways of my own mind..."

It did not matter, nor does it now when He seems distant and concerned, or when I am too wounded or preoccupied to believe He really knows or cares. Only in looking back can I begin to understand that each step along the way is part of a loving plan unfolding for my private joy and the service of any to whom I am sent. No one is superior or inferior, no matter the value judgments of caste or culture. Each of us is unique and custom-made, and every life is a private pathway to freedom and joy.

I cannot comprehend agonizing and constant suffering, or death that seems tragic and premature. I cannot understand the starvation of children, nor the despair of the lonely and tormented. Even when the pieces of my own life seem not to fit, or my most courageous and committed efforts are frustrated, I am often too angry or shattered to surrender to what is. Yet, I know there is a serene and silent pool of "quiet water in the center of my soul."

This is a book about my own inner odyssey, of the patient and gentle voice within that gradually leads me from anger and guilt, sadness and fear to trust and an abiding faith. But each of us must follow his own path, for each of us is guided in his own way. I do not impose my way on you, or mock the path that is yours. It does not matter whether we choose to chant in cathedrals or sit silently in forests, to bow in mosques and temples or walk the screaming city streets, ponder our scriptures or study the stars, laugh on mountains or weep in desolate valleys. Wherever we are, there is always quiet water in the center of our soul.

James Kavanaugh

In The Center Of Your Soul

There is quiet water
   In the center of your soul,
Where a son or daughter
   Can be taught what no man knows.

There's a fragrant garden
   In the center of your soul,
Where the weak can harden
   And a narrow mind can grow.

There's a rolling river
   In the center of your soul,
An eternal giver
   With a rich and endless flow.

There's a land of muses
   In the center of your soul,
Where the rich are losers
   And the poor are free to go.

So remain with me, then,
   To pursue another goal
And to find your freedom
   In the center of your soul.

Nothing Has Changed From Childhood

Nothing has changed from childhood,
    The same longing for peace,
    The same hope for final fulfillment.
Life could have been easier had there been teachers
    and wise men instead of drones imitating
    drones and parrots mimicking parrots.
If I were to begin again, I would challenge authority
    from the crib,
    Trust only smiles and laughter that echo across
        all darkness.
For years I puzzled over monks who left the world to
    hide in cloisters and ancient regulations.
At last I know that freedom is a curse save for the very
    brave,
    And I am only brave enough to wonder at the
        heavens.
Too many friends have died, too many stars are
    fallen,
Too many questions go unanswered.
Philosophers waste their time, even Augustine was
    grave too soon.
I would have loved him before his conversion.

There is too much pain in the world,
   Too much suffering without significance,
   Till finally I know that love alone is worth the
      price,
   Yet no one told me about love.

I was taught that conquests would fill the emptiness
   beneath the surface of my heart.
Now I am content to be Aesop, selling my fables for
   lunch money,
Satisfied to avoid black holes and galaxies,
   Staying close to frogs and flowers and the smell
      of baking bread.
I wander the slums of Beijing and Brazil, and know
   that staying alive is joy enough when the struggle
   is too fierce.
I woke this morning, wondering what was left to do,
   asking questions which only I can answer,
   Finally grateful to love with a wounded heart.
So, for today, I will survive, and for tomorrow,
   Because nothing has changed from childhood,
Except I no longer permit anyone beyond myself
   To tell me what to do.

The Script

We followed the script carefully through life
    Childhood dreams and football teams
    Walks in the woods
    And love on hay wagons.
We moved through college and professions
    Abrupt detours and humble confessions.
    Marriage and kids
    Even divorce and the pain
        that wouldn't go away.
We changed jobs,
    dreamed of mounting investments
    And every possible success,
    Chased hobbies and rainbows
    Made love and knew that it would
        all go on forever.
Each page of the script was numbered,
    few mysteries or difficult words,
Hurts enough and bleeding,
    but we hurried on, ignored the wounds
        and they went away.
Something always worked to hold us together.
Then one day, silently, suddenly,
    it all came apart,
And we turned the page and discovered
Nothing else had been written.
We were alone with blank pages,
    with our confusion and fear,
        With fleeting time and words
That had to be written privately, uniquely
    in the depths of our own hearts,
Without any script but our own!

Life Stretches Ahead

Life stretches ahead
Like some uncharted, winding gravel road
  Passing through hills and valleys
With unfamiliar scenery and disappearing
  landmarks.
Even loyal friends who have seen me through
  madness and mounting fears
  Cannot tell me which way to turn
  Or when to turn back at the threat of
    sudden storms.
Even my lover struggles to survive and cannot
  whisper comforting directions
  When dawn bursts on my consciousness,
    confusing me with its exaggerated
    splendor,
  Or darkness calms my torrent of fright,
    permitting me a momentary peace.
So I walk, step by step,
  Guided by sometimes friendly stars
  Washed by the wind and rain
  Chilled by the snow of mountain peaks
  Warmed by the desert's monotonous heat,
Trusting blindly that the gravel road will take
  me where I must go,
Hoping quietly that the unfamiliar scenery is
  only a friend dressed differently,
Loving gently all I meet along the way
  Where none who walks alone is ever a
    stranger,
As life stretches ahead.

Enough

Enough serenity and playing in the sun,
Enough pleasure and working to have fun.
Enough worry and the pursuit of things,
Enough leisure and the boredom it brings.
Enough success
  With the theft of every hour,
Enough investments
  With their artificial power.
Enough friends to organize my days,
Enough critics to analyze my ways.
Enough loneliness
Enough pain
Enough emptiness
Time to start again.

There Must Be An Easier Way

There must be an easier way
  To go about living.
    Some stone decalogue hidden at the roots of a tree,
    Some white-haired wise man at the crest of a hill,
    Some hoarse voice whispering in a dark confessional.
I always end up in the woods
  Making gentle love with a sycamore tree,
  Or telling funny stories to chipmunks,
  Or tracing my fingers across nipples of moss.
    —And taking advice only from the wind.

It's Time

It's time to clothe my dreams in reality,
To create a home for wanderers
Who cannot bow before the traditions of a
    single-family dwelling
And a fenced-in yard.
Who look beyond marriage and blood
To gather brothers and sisters tied by more than
    custom and umbilical cords.
Generous minds and loving hearts,
    laughing eyes and simple tastes,
Who know that serenity at sunrise and peace
    at sunset
Are worth more than the treasuries of kings and
    IRA security.

It's time to clothe my dreams in reality,
    To gather together kindred spirits
    Who look beyond what is and was
        To understand what can be,
    Who know that love and compassion, joy and
        peace are our birthright
    Stolen by a culture's madness and to band
        together the manipulations of frightened
        lives,
        wise minds and bruised hearts,
    Daring souls and brave spirits
    Who know that love is worth the stars
    And friendship does not hide its private
        anxieties behind sophistication and
        steel symbols.

It's time to clothe my dreams in reality,
To move beyond jealousy and possession,
   isolation and imprisonment,
To confront boredom and loneliness,
   sadness and lovelessness,
To make known my secret needs and reveal my
   hidden yearnings,
To risk self-exposure as the only path to final
   freedom,
To surround myself with the energy flowing from
   the earth's core,
The passion of rivers and the resilience of trees,
And thus to clothe my dreams in reality!

Of Childhood Dreams

No one need abandon childhood dreams that
     outlive dry illusions
  Born of fear and other's hoarded expectations.
There is but one lesson to learn, as easy as squirrels
     and sunshine,
A lesson echoed endlessly in whispers in the
     sanctuary of your heart,
  No matter how long or far you have strayed.
To ignore it is the only sin, a tragic guarantee that
  Sadness and emptiness will haunt the final days
     of your life.
Though the mountains fall on you and the sky
     denies her light,
Though the moon disappear and clouds are
     troubled and angry,
All of this will pass away no matter
     the time or season.

Then the dreams you refused to abandon will
     explode with new life.
  Taller than the mountains, brighter
     than the sun,
And the joyful song that was yours from
     the beginning
Will resound across the silver edges of your
     days and nights,
And lead you lovingly and fearlessly into the light.

Some Walk Through Life

Some walk through life with no monuments
    For anyone to admire.
Not a house built or a child,
    Not a city reconstructed or an apple tree.
Content with some vague freedom.

  There are enough lovers,
    Enough creators and artists, but
Not enough who live their own lives
    And walk strong against the sky
      Without murdering or expecting,
      Calculating or dissecting,
Just drifting along without plans.
No noble causes or sudden losses,
    No wise words or sprawling herds,
Ready to die along some dusty street,
    If so it must be.
Some ego centered deep inside
    And a rare appreciation for life
Without clever definitions or subtle ambitions
Knowing
  That there are enough trees and clever men,
  That's it's time to clear the land and walk
  Going nowhere,
    Content
    Withal
    To be.

You Are Light And Love

You are light and love,
   No matter what echoes have said or are saying still--
      Of parents sealed in their own tomb
         of childhood pain,
      Of spouses spewing self hatred in gathered vials
         of poisonous words,
      Of a guilt producing God made carefully
         in the image of angry and self loathing men,
      Of authorities damning, neighbors ranting, hated
         jobs failing as an invitation to creativity and joy,
   Despite the litany of self appointed critics whose
      judgment has no valid currency.

You are light and love,
   No matter what your ruminations said or are saying still--
      Of the hoarded self contempt that mercilessly
         condemns a frightened, struggling child within,
      Of judgments inherited, blame assumed, and
         the sentence passed,
      Of broken marriages, angry offspring, and hidden
         loneliness that never leaves,
      Of children gone awry or parents distant
         and disappointed,
   Despite resolutions discarded, promises broken, and
      lifelong lies finally passing as truth.

You are light and love, God's own child,
    A unique and wondrous design, worthy of all
        reverence and respect,
    Deserving above all of your own most precious love
        that gradually inflames your entire being
    So that the light and love you finally know you are,
        shines forth to illuminate a weary world and
        its wounded children,
With the reflected love and light that glows
    Within your own soul!

All The Joy In The World

All the joy in the world takes possession of me today,
   Unending nights and darkened
    days forgotten,
   Failures and unplanned frustrations,
     rejections and angry confrontations
     have lost their power.
   Deserting friends I once missed,
   Bitter enemies I once feared,
   Promises never kept and dreams unrealized
    Seem as nothing.
The sky belongs to me and the birds are assembled in
   concert only for my ears,
Each towering tree, shaped by storms and time into
   some impossible symmetry, is for my eyes alone.
The mountains, clear against the heavens, are my
   personal delight,
The day is my private extravagance
   And I alone can ravish and enjoy the night.

My own company satisfies, my own thoughts an
   immeasurable treasure,
The breeze is music enough, bubbling streams
   drama enough,
I make my own happiness and create my own
   climate and weather.
I am a stranger nowhere, an alien no place on sea
   or planet,
   Forever at home in my world.
God is everywhere, love abounds, energy explodes
   without prompting,
   And I am grateful for every moment of my
      life,
Grateful most of all to be completely,
   irrevocably alive!

Stubby

Stubby has more confidence with less reason than
    anyone I've ever known,
He's thirty pounds overweight,
    works ten hours a week,
    Spends more time traveling than the pope,
And he's as comfortable with a beggar
    as a diplomat.
On an exclusive tennis court, he wore khaki pants,
    three-dollar shoes, and an Hawaiian shirt,
    returned maybe ten balls in two sets
    and told me later he thinks his game
        is getting stronger.
He laughs at everything, eats what he wants,
    and will break any appointment.
His family background is gravied with everything
    from alcoholic parents to child abuse
        and total neglect.
His saga reads like a TV documentary on how lives
    are destroyed.
While I worry, and wonder and check my psyche
    assiduously,
    he picks up grateful ladies
        at assorted night spots.

He would play golf with Arnold Palmer without
   embarrassment and shoot 162,
      sing at a bar, though he's totally tone deaf,
      and dance with anyone
      always using the same two-step shuffle.
He contradicts everything I've ever read in
   theology, psychology, and anthropology.
Either he's got the damndest genes
Or he's the one successful lobotomy that left
   everything but gloom, fear,
         and insecurity intact.
If that's the case, I'm looking for the same doctor!

Once I Smiled

Once I smiled like a summer breeze
Even in winter,
Until the seasons of my life
Were as monotonous
As the soft clouds and blue skies
Of Hawaii and the Caribbean.
I was a travel bureau
Denying rain and hurricane,
Apologizing for the sudden storms
That came rarely.

Now a menacing cloud
Can interrupt the placid days,
A lashing wind awakens palm trees
And covers the beach with flotsam.
The sea leaps before me
And tourists take cover in grass huts.
Lights dim and radios rasp,
The birds pull in their wings
And the heavens open up
In unrelenting deluge.

Then there is quiet after the storm,
The birds return to tease the tourists,
And my smile is as warm and real
As the gentle, cleansing rain.

Walk Easy On The Earth

Walk easy on the earth
   Each life has its own fragile rhythm,
   To be aware of it is to understand,
   To ignore it is to abandon oneself to sadness.
   It is to search vainly for the wholeness
      that only comes in surrender to what is.

Walk easy on the earth
   Too much seriousness obscures beauty,
   Intensity blinds and distorts one's focus,
   Excessive ambition destroys true perception.
   It is not hard work or suffering that debilitates,
      but a loss of contact with oneself.

Walk easy on the earth
   Anger clouds vision and rage shortens life,
   Laughter is the greatest gift of the free spirit.
   To laugh profoundly and often is to understand,
   To laugh at oneself and all of life,
      and thus to see clearly.

Walk easy on the earth
   Love is waiting to reveal itself when it is time,
   Nor can one create it despite the most noble intent.
   Love is the discovery of one's own rhythm in another.
   Any other love, regardless of time or commitment,
      will only be doomed and painful.

This above all. Walk easy on the earth!

The Time Came

The time came when all that is merely human failed,
    And the best efforts of medics and wise men with
        all the tools of two thousand years of trying
Came to nought. I was cut adrift from myself,
    destined to wither
    If I could not salvage a suitable reason to live,
Finally cut off from the omnipotence of parental help,
Finally segregated from the abundant generosity of
    friends,
Finally having exhausted the relief that the centuries
    had garnered from the vials and occult theories
    of civilization's finest minds.
There were no relieving drugs or miracles, no
    soothing words enough or clever theorems.
Only the simple words I heard as a child of a God
    Who cared
    And could make a blind man see for no reason
        save love.
So I sought Him in simplicity and fear, perhaps in
    desperation,
    More in doubt than faith, more in faltering
    words than bold eloquence.
I offered Him my energies all the days of my life if He
    would but attend my pleading, bring back the
    joy of morning, the serenity of the trees, the
    soothing resonance of sunset.

I asked not fame or power, security or success, only
    the wholeness that every other recourse had
    denied me.
Softly He spoke, not in Sinai's thunder or Noe's rain,
    not in transcending light upon a mountain, nor
    even in a whispered call along the shores of
    Galilee.
He only spoke of patience and enough time, of
    listening to the day and attending the night,
That wholeness would come when my heart was pure
    again,
And my aspirations were those of a child grown to
    manhood.

Somewhere Along The Way

Somewhere along the way
A persistent voice taught me I was in competition
  With every other man in the world.
I listened carefully
  And learned the lesson well.

It was not enough
  To find a loving wife and have average,
    happy kids,
  To see a sunrise and wonder at an
    eclipsing moon,
  To enjoy a meal and catch a trout in a silent,
    silver river,
  To picnic in a meadow at the top of a mountain
    Or ride horses along the rim of a hidden lake,
  To laugh like a child at midnight
    And to still wonder about the falling stars.

It was only enough
  To be admired and powerful and to rush from
    one success to another,
  To barely see faces or hear voices, to ignore beauty
    and forget about music,

To reduce everything and everybody to a stereo color
   pattern on the way to some new triumph,
To rest in no victory, but to create new and more
   demanding goals even as I seem to succeed,
Until finally I was estranged and exhausted,
   victorious and joyless,
   successful and ready to abandon life.

Then somewhere along the way
   I remembered the laugh of a child I once knew,
   I saw a familiar boy wandering joyously
      in the woods,
   I felt a heart pounding with excitement at
      the birth of a new day,
   Until I was in competition with no one and life
      was clear again,
Somewhere along the way.

When The Pain Is More Acute Than You Can Bear

When the pain is more acute than you can bear,
And you are convinced that no one in the world
    suffers as much,
When the morning is as opaque as night and the
    dawn but a discordant alarm, announcing yet
    another bitter struggle to survive,
When a bird's song to the day or the serene
    murmuring of a dove
    cannot draw your mind from feeding on itself,
Clinging like some wretched scavenger to drain out
    joy and wonder,
When the soft light of daybreak cannot distract or the
    gently shimmering of the locust leaves cannot
    inspire,
When even the shrill cries of summer children are but
    screams that echo in some mad corridor of
    consciousness,
Know that you are not dying, but preparing to enter
    another level of life,
A level beyond avarice and fleeting fame, beyond
    servile dependence on opinions or words of
    praise,
Beyond power and mastery and control, beyond
    jealousy and competition,
Beyond lust and greed and insatiable ambition, a
    level where joy flows from simplicity and love,
From some rhythm shared with trees and flowers and
    circling planets.

Then all the pain is as nothing, rather a choice and
    heavenly messenger sent like some ancient
    angel of the East
To announce a more profound and solid way to
    self-esteem and serenity.
Thus pain is not an enemy, but a friend who promises
    to take you where peace abides,
Who leads you beyond bitterness to abandon specious
    and empty pursuits, hollow and ill-founded
    hopes, destructive and untimely dreams,
Until you walk in the world freer and more joyful
    than ever before,
Less anxious and less frightened of death,
    one with life,
In an harmonious accord,
    Bred of suffering, of annihilation,
    Bred of emptiness and frustration,
And leading directly and inexorably to a true
    and genuine,
    An eternal and purified self.

So Often

So often I stand like a bashful child,
    Speechless before those I love,
Wanting to tell them all that is in my heart,
But frightened by some distance in their eyes.
Thus, so much of life is lived all alone,
    So many conversations with one's self go
      unanswered.
I would like to begin again, do it all right this time.
    There would be no docile, frightened adolescent,
      Smiling endlessly to hide his anger
      Trampling on his own fears
      Ignoring his private dreams
      Fighting for some recognition that never
        came from within.
No one could push or prod me,
No one could intimidate or smother me,
No one could drive me to adore a God
    I didn't understand.
Strange! Even as a little boy I knew it was all wrong,
    That life was far more than docility and duty
      and self-annihilation!
All these years spent reclaiming that child who was
    instinctively wiser than all his teachers,
All these years spent trying to recapture what I
    surrendered to frightened preachers,
Until I can only ask that the loving, prodigal child
    who was lost will finally reappear,
So that life is the circle it was meant to be,
    That the child who flowered at life's beginning
    Will once more flourish at its end.

I Asked The River

I asked the river
    Where he was going
        and how he would know
        when he got there.
He only laughed at me
    Splashing across the rocks.

I asked the mountain
    When he was high enough
        and how he would know
        when he reached the heavens.
His echo only laughed
    Like thunder in the valleys.

I asked the trees
    How long they would live
        and how they would know
        when they were a forest
There leaves only shook with mirth
    In the joy of a sudden wind storm.

Finally I was silent,
    As if there were no one else to please,
And I spent my time laughing
    With the river, the mountain,
        and trees.

My Easy God Is Gone

I have lost my easy God—the one whose name
    I knew since childhood.
I knew his temper, his sullen outrage, his
    ritual forgiveness.
I knew the strength of his arm, the sound
    of his insistent voice.
His beard bristling, his lips full and red
    with moisture at the moustache,
His eyes clear and piercing, too blue
    to understand all,
His face too unwrinkled to feel my
    child's pain.
He was a good God—so he told me—
    a long suffering and manageable one.
I knelt at his feet and kissed them,
    I felt the smooth countenance
    of his forgiveness.

I never told him how he frightened me,
    How he followed me as a child
When I played with friends or begged
    for candy on Halloween.
He was a predictable God, I was the
    unpredictable one.
He was unchanging, omnipotent, all-seeing,
    I was volatile and helpless.
He taught me to thank him for the concern
    which gave me no chance to breathe,
For the love which demanded only love in
    return—and obedience.
He made pain sensible and patience possible
    and the future foreseeable.

He, the mysterious, took all mystery away,
        corroded my imagination,
Controlled the stars and would not let
        them speak for themselves.

Now he haunts me seldom, some fierce
        umbilical is broken,
I live with my own fragile hopes and
        sudden rising despair.
Now I do not weep for my sins, I have
        learned to love them
And to know that they are the wounds that
        make love real.
His face eludes me, his voice, with all
        its pity, does not ring in my ear.
His maxims memorized in boyhood do not
        make fruitless and pointless my experience.
I walk alone, but not so terrified as when
        he held my hand.
I do not splash in the blood of his son
        nor hear the crunch of nails or thorns
        piercing protesting flesh.
I am a boy again—I whose boyhood was
        turned to manhood in a brutal myth.
Now wine is only wine with drops that do
        not taste of blood.
The bread I eat has too much pride for transubstantiation,
        I too—and together the bread and I embrace,
Each grateful to be what we are, each loving
        from our own reality.
Now the bread is warm in my mouth and
        I am warm in its mouth as well.

Now my easy God is gone—he knew too
    much to be real,
He talked too much to listen, he knew
    my words before I spoke.
But I knew his answers as well—computerized
    and turned to dogma
His stamp was on my soul, his law locked
    cross-like on my heart,
His imperatives tattooed on my breast, his
    aloofness canonized in ritual.
Now he is gone—my easy, stuffy God—God,
    the father-master, the mother-whiner, the
Dull, whoring God who offered love bought
    by an infant's fear.
Now the world is mine with all its pain and
    warmth, with its every color and sound;
The setting sun is my priest with the ocean
    for its altar.
The rising sun redeems me with the rolling
    waves warmed in its arms.
A dog barks and I weep to be alive, a
    cat studies me and my joy is boundless.
I lie on the grass and boy-like, search the sky.
    The clouds do not turn to angels, the winds
    do not whisper of heaven or hell.

Perhaps I have no God—what does it matter?
    I have beauty and joy and transcending loneliness,
I have the beginning of love—as beautiful as it
    is feeble—as free as it is human.
I have the mountains that whisper secrets
    held before men could speak,

I have the ocean that belches life on
    the beach and caresses it in the sand,
I have a friend who smiles when he sees
    me, who weeps when he hears my pain,
I have a future full of surprises, a
    present full of wonder.
I have no past—the steps have disappeared
    the wind has blown them away.

I stand in the Heavens and on earth, I
    feel the breeze in my hair.
I can drink to the North Star and shout
    on a bar stool,
I can feel the teeth of a hangover, the
    joy of laziness,
The flush of my own rudeness, the surge of
    my own ineptitude.
And I can know my own gentleness as well,
    my wonder, my nobility.
I sense the call of creation, I feel its
    swelling in my hands.
I can lust and love, eat and drink, sleep
    and rise,
But my easy God is gone—and in his stead
    the mystery of loneliness and love!

No More Angry Gods

No more angry gods for me tossing thunderbolts
    like frisbees!
No more stone-eyed preachers threatening eternal
    lakes of fire!
No more bloody, atoning crucifixions to coat
    the innocent in guilt!
No more hostile words making Jesus the sacred bile
    of buried rage!
No more bibles spewing venom from rabid tongues
    of private fury!
No more bitter verses teaching frothing hate and
    gnashing teeth!
I want gods who can love and laugh from
    morning till night,
Laugh till the days skip and frolic, and weeks fall
    giggling over months and years.
I want to be saved from greed and avarice and
    good investments,
Saved from anger and fear, from courts
      and hostile words
  That drain my life and leave no patch of
      ground to walk on
In a world grown dark and grey, where the news is
    beyond enduring!
Life was meant to be joyful, work expressive
    of the best I am,
God attendant to my needs, and angels to guide me
    from all harm.
Can I go back and do it again? Feel what I feel, and
    find love for whatever I happen to do or be?

I want to lead an army of laughing people across
   freeways and over the hills,
Rid the world of gloom and despair, loneliness and
   unkind words!
I want to form a parade that marches beyond sad stories
   and human tragedy!
Finally I understand that the man from Galilee knew a
   better way of simplicity and love.
A pity his spokesmen still turn joy and promises into
   the lot of a galley slave!
And more the pity
   he does not return to start again
And clarify!

Surrender

Surrender to what is and love yourself
   in innocence—
Knowing that a benign spirit
   lives within you
And each cycle of life will pass
   as you move forward
To the joy and serenity that were
   always meant to be you!
Live beyond concern and fear,
   knowing that love is stronger than
   any of these impostors.
There is nothing to be afraid of,
Light is at every moment within your reach
   As you grow towards what you
     were eternally meant to be,
      and already are from childhood.

Surrender to what is and love yourself in
   innocence—
The pain will disappear in the light.
And the power that is yours,
   Beyond ambition or false security,
Will fill your being with peace
   That nothing else can give
There is an energy that you
   have never known, that flows
   like the tide and the
     gentle motion of clouds.
You will never again be alone
   for the light is your constant companion,
As you surrender to what is
And love yourself in innocence.

The Quiet Mornings

I like the quiet mornings
When the waves have washed the footprints
    from the shore,
When even the gulls are just beginning to stir
And the heat of the day has not yet aroused the flies
    to search the seaweed for breakfast,
When the beach still has the sand of sleep in its eyes
And the driftwood looks like tired swimmers
    resting on the shore
When the waves laugh at the rocks
And playfully wash the night from their eyes.

Soon enough the hungry gulls will dive for fish
And the waves will beat shape into the rocks.
Feet will pound on the beach
And ladies will snatch the driftwood for lamps,
And I will face the day's demands,
Trampled like the sand,
Wounded like the rocks,
Torn up like the wood,
Living for another quiet morning!

Man-Child

Beyond plans of success and dreams of affluence,
  Beyond threats and boasts and seeming confidence,
I see your fear and know that when you
        lose your boyhood,
You lose what makes you warm and attractive as a man.

Life is not lived in spurts
  Where manhood destroys boyhood like some
    major surgery never to be undone.
I love not your obvious triumphs and
        heady expertise,
  But a laughing, playful, awkward boy,
        unchained and unpredictable,
        who can drop everything to hear
  A distant seal trumpeting on the midnight rocks,
Or watch the messy swallow building his mortared nest,
  Fouling picture windows and garage doors
    like a demented mason.
When the boy is gone, the man is all drive and head,
  Without arms and legs, without eyes and ears and
    some explosive joy.

There is no life as fine as spontaneity and passion.
  No success to match a vibrant energy of life,
And assuredly, none more beautiful than
        one who moves
  Bravely beyond the hungry needs of boyhood,
To stay in daily, loving contact with his inner child.

There Were Days

There were days when I wanted the world
    to know that I was alive,
As important as men of power and letters,
As significant a cultural force as names
    in distant textbooks.
I wanted acknowledgement and homage,
    respect and applause.
Now I only want to wake up and see the sky,
    To know that I walk the world joyfully
        like the simple ones of earth.
I want smiles and laughter, flowers
    and a silent meditation by the sea.
I want friends who love me as I am,
    with all my fears and faults,
Who love my very being and presence
    were I never to write a word,
Or achieve anything beyond enjoying the sun
    and the face of a child.
    If life is not serenity, it is nothing,
    If life is not peace, it is warfare.
I have had enough war, enough strife,
    now I look for
    Simplicity and friendship and quiet times,
Satisfied that my power is in the God
    Who lives in my soul
    And directs me as He will,
Until I love only what He wants
    and live as He has destined
Me to live.

Only One Mistake To Be Made

There's only one mistake to be made:
   Not to be who you really are!
Power can confuse you and friends who want
   Not you, but what you can provide,
   Even as they are unwilling or unable
     To comprehend your heart.
I have been at the top and the bottom,
Rode the roller coaster with the best
And groveled in misery with the worst
   of our race.
I have leaped from bed to make the world
   salute my presence,
And pulled the covers over my head to hide
   from my own assorted fears.
In the process I have learned that
I am as fragile as an acorn in the grasp
   of a hungry, lusting squirrel,
And as strong as the ocean that refuses,
   despite storms and shipwrecks,
To cease beating relentlessly against the shore.
I've learned to admire, more than rank or pedigree,
Those wanderers and wayfarers I've known, even
   proud and bearded vagabonds,
Who can still walk the earth as owners,
And have little to fear that has not
   already happened.

Even death is but a step along the way,
And the thought of slipping away without
   Doctor or companion, family or friend
     does not intimidate.
Such, by whatever strange and circuitous path,
Have found some God deep within themselves,
   A God beyond theologies and definition,
   A God as strong and fragile as they are,
   A God Who finally revealed Himself when
     there was no place else to turn,
A God Who loves them because, far more than I,
They have become who they really are!

Ernie

There's gotta be a law against a guy like Ernie,
I mean, one drink
  And he's the happiest sonofabitch in the world.
It just ain't right
  To drive a delivery truck most of your life,
  To be married three times
    And to have kids by four different women,
  Not to know your father
    And to call your mother once or twice a year,
  To greet whores and nuns, kids and councilmen
    With the same broad grin,
  To ignore church and never to have opened a Bible,
    Or even wondered about it,
  Not to fear death
    And have no opinions about an afterlife,
  To think the sun, moon, stars, and a summer day
    Are your private endowment,
And to be the happiest sonofabitch in the world
  After just one drink.

If The Mountain

If mountains lose their splendor
  And flowers smile unseen,
If rivers gasp in boredom,
  And summer's hardly green.
If meadows do not lure me,
  And night's forever chill,
If floating clouds can't cure me,
  And forests lose their spell.
If the moon is but a stranger
  And the golden dawn is gone,
If the dark won't whisper secrets,
  And the birds forget their song,
Then it's time to ease ambition,
  And rest my frantic brain,
To hear my spirit's warnings,
  The loving words of pain.

It's time to seek another path,
  To bid the past "Goodbye!"
Until my feet are dipped in dirt,
  My head floats in the sky.
For I am born of sun and sand,
  Of water, sky, and air,
And if I seem to lose my life,
  It's waiting for me there.
I'll shun the distant roll of drums
  Where captive crowds applaud,
And crawl along the unmarked road
  To find my way to God!

Let Go Of It All

Let go of it all and see where it takes you.
Let the money slide away and the tense young men
  Who talk of security and conquests.
Let the cars whiz by, the square jaws and
  too bright eyes
Stumble and fall and lie prone upon the earth
  Until you taste the dirt again and make friends
    with the fog.
Toss your plans aboard the first wind heading north
  And your ambitions on a breeze heading south.
Let it all descend upon you like lava and sunshine
And let the clouds guide you as they will.
There is no mountain high enough to climb
    with satisfaction,
  No hole deep enough to dig, no ocean vast
    enough to cross.
There is only laughter and peace and
    the present moment,
  Your breath in unison with the throbbing earth,
  Your flight as aimless and transient as the birds.
Let it all go and wash you like the rain,
Let it all go and buffet you like the wind,
Let it all go and see where it takes you
  Until you are one with the earth
    and all its inhabitants.

For One Unafraid To Be Himself

There is no failure for one unafraid to be himself,
No defeat for one who does what he can without
    sacrificing the private rhythm of his being,
A rhythm created over centuries and shared
    with life itself.
Failure is only a chance to begin again,
Defeat but a gentle warning to walk another road,
Loneliness an invitation to find a new friend.
A life built on sand and avarice is the victim
    of every earthquake or avalanche,
Every rise and fall of Dow Jones or a robot's dictation.
Wrap yourself in your own feeble being,
Warm yourself with your own fragile heart,
Defend yourself in peace and silence, and do battle
    with smiles and shrugs
And an awareness of eternal change.
Patience and humility are your impermeable armor,
Love and prayer your impregnable protection.
Your worst adversary is crippled with everyman's fears,
The most severe critic but a raconteur of his own story.
How can there be failure when the ocean still rolls
    towards the land?
And the night still embraces strong and weak alike
    with love?
The morning will come with its soft light
    to offer you a childhood again,
And the wind will sing the gentle rhythm that makes
    of each day a new adventure.

One Little Man

One little man making his way in a frightening world,
    Frightening only if he walks all by himself,
Or listens to the hollowness of his own wounded heart.
The only strength is to let go, walking openly with God
    As He gently reveals Himself the way He chooses.
Even now as the Bhuddist priest says his daily prayers
    At some far and undistinguished corner of the earth,
As a meek charwoman of Mecca looks radiantly to the sun,
    And the man of Israel or Ireland seeks his own peace,
A God beyond Sinai and Pentecost, beyond words and icons
    Bends to bless and heal, to make brave and serene.
The freedom that power and possessions cannot provide,
    Is freely given to the little ones in the darkest
        corners of the earth,
If only they are trusting child enough to ask!

Gentle Old Woman

Gentle old woman with her shopping bag
Shuffling through Woolworth's to find a little yarn
   —just the right shade of purple—
To hold her flowered hat in an unfriendly wind.
"I almost lost it twice," she tells me,
"And I thought it was a goner under the
   Greyhound bus."
Fragile as a desert's fast-departing flower
Wrinkled with memories and spotted like a child
   freckled in the sun
Chuckling softly at her own feebleness,
Finally satisfied with the delicate purple of a
   Jacaranda tree.
"Not too tight," she tells me,
"No sense croaking before my time."
Hat in place, crowned with faded flowers,
She extracts three pennies from deep within her
   beaded purse, still determined to pay her way.
I hold the heavy door,
And watch her shuffle, still chuckling
   into the wind,
Climbing her own Everest,
Winning her own Olympics,
Solving the day's problem with just the
   right shade of purple.

I Sometimes Remember

I sometimes remember amid the paper and the
  evening news
    That it was those powerful executives and politicians,
      Charming and insensitive,
      Logical and persevering,
      Confident and ruthless
Who built the cars we drive
  The planes and computers,
  Skyscrapers and hospitals,
  Space capsules and TVs
  Railroads and iron lungs and artificial hearts.
And I try to remember that they were probably not unlike
  The discoverers of new continents
  And the explorers of uncharted lands
    and unknown seas.
But I also remember that it was the same kind of men
  Stress-filled and calculating
  Unscrupulous and conniving,
    Who started the pointless wars we fought
    The depressions and revolutions,
    The famines and slavery,
    The atrocities and plagues,
    The poverty and starvation and private despair,
      Of the fragile and disenfranchised.
Then I remember that it was the same kind of men
  —for whatever reason—
  Who ended the wars they began
  And solved the problems they created
  Even as they plotted to create even more.
All of which makes me wonder if we weren't better off
  Working by hand
  Traveling by foot
And listening to the music of the wind.

I'm Gonna Sit Here

I'm gonna sit here
    Till passion returns
    And tells me where to go.
I don't care if it's heaven
    Or hell or home,
I don't care if it's work
    Or play or sex,
I don't care if it's rich
    Or poor or madness,
I don't even care
    If it's riding a white horse naked
    on a freeway
    Or lining up like we did as kids
        For a pissing contest in the old
        schoolyard.
I'm not going anywhere
    - even to death -
Until I can go passionately.

When I Grey

When I grey, I want the young to laugh and
        ask questions,
    I want deer to nibble grass by the lake
        at twilight,
    And mallards to circle my pond cautiously
        at sunrise.
    I want to gaze at mountains I have climbed
    And dream of all the cities I have seen
        at midnight.
    I want to remember every love like
        a friendly landscape,
    And write the stories I had forgotten
        in life's haste,
    I want to sit with you in silence, share a
        thousand dreams without a word.
    I want to be friends with the whole world
        and a gentle guest of all the universe.

Most of all, when I grey,
    I want to be grateful for every breath,
    Forgiving of every least injury,
    Mindful of everyone I've hurt and thankful
        for everyone who ever loved me.

When I grey,
    I want the days to blend softly into night,
    The darkness to surrender patiently
        to dawn.
    I want to shout the history of my joys
        from hilltops.
    And sing a new and passionate and
        never-ending song.
    I want to laugh with lifelong friends
        at table,
    To exaggerate our triumphs
        drinking wine,
    I want to write as long as I am able,
    And thank the household gods
        that you are mine,

When I grey.

My Sadness Has No Seasons

My sadness has no seasons,
It comes when the leaves
    Surrender to the persistent wind
    And lie at attention,
When the snow
    Coats twigs and footprints
    In a gentle obituary of white,
Or when the birds
    Fly back to the parks
    To help the old folks count the years.
It even comes when the hot air
    Keeps the crickets awake,
    Complaining in the parched grass.

There are no reasons for my sadness
    Except living, and maybe dying.
But mostly it moves in like the fog,
Seeping from some secret cave where shadows live.

I wish I were a planet so my sadness would have seasons,
If it came with sun or snow, I'd somehow know its reasons.

Finding The Courage

Finding the courage to face some buried anxiety
   As real as snakes and grizzly bears in an
      uncharted wilderness,
Struggling in vain to recall a child's overpowering
   fear
   Still rooted deeply in my flesh
   And seemingly as impermeable as granite rocks.
When was that terrifying moment that has
   Left its shadows till now?
What was the dagger that carved a scar never to be
   erased?
   Was I seven or seventeen, infant or fragile
      adolescent?
Vainly I recall every angry, hurtful voice
   of childhood,
   Every silent attack of parent or peer, teacher
      or coach.
Who wounded me when my bones were too brittle to
   bear the weight?
   When my mind was too timid and unformed to
      fight back?
How can I battle this elusive Hydra
   With its hybrid and devouring teeth?
Will I carry the last of this struggle to my grave?
   Will it reappear to torture me at the very end?
Or will the sun finally rise some glorious morning
   And the roots of an ancient fear dissolve like
      the disappearing night?

To Give Each Reality

To give each reality its own identity,
   And not mine.
To rejoice in the color of a chair,
   The bloom of a rug, the gentle warmth of a lamp.
To see the compassionate eyes of a dog,
   The curious eyes of a cat,
   The innocent, frightened ones of a rabbit,
And to know that they are their own being.
To see dawn as its own glory and the moon
      as its own splendor,
The day and night as neighbors, possessed of
      their own being beyond any delight of mine.
To see you as fragile and strong, as hungry
      and well nourished,
As your own essence and not a reflection of mine.
To rejoice in you for what you are
   And not for what you bring to me.

Then finally to see myself for what I am
   And not for what others want me to be,
Not even for what my fears and vanity
   Would fashion me to be.
This is to be free, to be totally alive,
   This, above all, is to love!

The Healing

The healing of the deepest wounds seems slow,
But time is of little consequence for all the joys
    that lie ahead.
So much time spent walking through life, going where
    you never were.
Now, at last you are alive in each moment,
Taught by pain and the lonely separation from yourself.
Once you wanted it all, now you know that all
    lives in each honest moment.
Excitement and exuberant echoes are no match
    for serenity and gentle peace,
A contented heart, a trusted friend, and finally time
    to look long enough to see.
It is a loving God Who hands you a custom cup to drink,
A brave and loving man who drinks it all and lives.
    Take back the eyes that were blinded by hurry
        and preoccupation!
    Take back the ears that were deafened by
        discordant sounds!
    Take back the words that only echoed in the wind!
Now you are your own, and patient healing will teach you
    What no master ever did or could.

All These Years

It took me all these years to lay a foundation,
To find mortar and bricks, level land and an acre
    all my own.
Now I will place each pillar of support cautiously
    and firmly,
Simplify my elaborate architectural plans,
Content with a single room, securely roofed, that
    is warm and friendly and mine.
Now I am no longer who I thought I was,
    Designer of palaces and mansions,
Master of light and power and rising towers
    of affluence and success.
I am only what I always was, a kid from Kalamazoo
    who sold magazines and peddled papers,
    mowed grass and transplanted bushes
Chopped down weeds and watered flowers.
But I will have my house, smaller than I imagined,
But finally all mine, where I can hide and emerge,
    laugh and reflect and light soft flickering candles
        as beautiful as any
    cathedral or elaborate estate.
There are music and books, food and warmth and
    light, and a friend or two who grin at my
        jokes and look at me with
    love and respect beyond any possibility of loss
    or remission.
They know and I know—and it does not matter if
    it took all these years to lay a foundation.

Hey Life!

Hey life!
Is this all you offer
With your circles of sameness
And petty goals giving ulcers to the ambitious,
Your promise of love and meaning and joy,
Your fictitious payoff?

Hey life!
I have seen the somber faces of your children
With a desert's emptiness etched thereon in sadness.
Liquor gives them joy—or a passing romance,
Or a kingdom that offers affluence and fear—
The sun is not enough.

Hey life!
Men drown themselves in conquests and payments,
Women are content to rest submerged in fantasy.
Hatred is as meaningful as hobbies,
Greed gives energy and fear responsibility,
And guilt is fuel enough!

Hey life!
Philosophers stumble and search for meaning,
Studying the heavens to comfort the earth.
There is no comfort—only time to serve,
There is no prison—save that which man makes
And offers to another.

Hey life!
Man is the obedient animal, obedient to you.
He challenges the earth to release its metals
And the heavens to explore its stars.
Only you elude him and mock him
And offer concentric circles.

Hey life!
The pilgrims kept busy, the Christians prayed,
The Jews postponed victory and vengeance like
Communists,
Cowards went mad to live as children,
Soldiers hid their pain to win medals,
But most men are vampires.

Hey life!
Man lives never knowing what it means,
Contented by a dash of pleasure and the screams.
His joy—but a moment's respite from pain,
His victory—to know that he is not slain
And can have children!

Hey life!
I see your mocking smile
That hovers over sadness in scorn
Without ever sharing it or even seeing it.
I have no time for you—only for man
Who outlives you!

I Have Walked

I have walked in lands where there are no paths
  or footprints,
No guided tours or warnings posted
  for the unsuspecting,
Where visas are denied and passports
        have no validity.
  Lands frozen with monsters of childhood
    and strange museums of assorted horrors.
  Lands of flowers with dark, staring eyes,
    and trees with gaunt, grasping fingers,
    Sullen lands where silence lives and ancient fears
      blow from nowhere like the wind,
  Where men and women stand alone
    amid darkness and sinister visions
        beyond all retelling.
I go there when someone demands it, despite tears
  and fears that I cannot survive another visit.
I return when an unseen hand mercifully opens
  a healing door and plead like a child
    in the hope I have finally escaped.
But perhaps I must go there again and again
  Until I am brave enough to bring
    light to the flowers' eyes and warmly shake
      the hands of the frightening trees.
Thus to create light in darkness, as a true child of
  God with power and courage
    granted only to those few
Who are admitted to the lands
  without paths or footprints
And love finally confronts loneliness
    at its core.

When It All Gets Too Heavy

Days when it all gets too heavy
I drift away to the sea
Or where the sunshine filters through trees,
And strip away my clothes,
Let go of everything I own,
    Everything I hope to be,
    Everything others have hoped for me.
Till I feel some connection
    With the earth
    And sun,
Some profound contact
    With the sky
    And water,
I lie for hours almost motionless
    Laugh at ambition
    Know that most pain
        Is the by-product of my plans
        The weight of my expectations.

Then for a time I am free again
I can feel my smile
    In my hands and my knees,
    Spreading over my cheeks,
    Softening my face
    And warming my groin.
I walk slowly and talk slowly,
    Move with the trees,
    Feel the grass growing up my legs,
    The wind blowing like my very blood,
    My body flowing with the planet.
And for a time I know
    I am rooted in the earth
    That nothing will take away my life
Unless I give my heart
    To those who have never kissed a tree
    Or made love with a soft green hill.

You Are Your Own Answer

You are your own answer,
    Beyond books and seers,
        psychics or doctors
    Beyond the strength that comes
        from what you have accomplished.
Your weakness is as valuable as your strength,
Your helplessness as loveable as your charm.
You are God's child and each step of the way,
    He gives you bread and not a stone,
        food and not a serpent.
All is part of the plan, as you look within
    And listen to the quiet, persistent voice
        that tells you who you are.
There is no strength greater than yours.
    No wisdom not available to you.
And love and light will flood your being
When you believe deeply enough to know
    that you are your own answer
In the beauty and creativity that make us all one.
No one beyond our love, no one not connected.
Abandon anger and fear to the wind,
    sadness and pseudo-strength to the earth.
Be who you are, in whatever state,
    and you will discover
That you are your own answer
    in the silence of your heart.
Where all light and power dwell forever.

Laughing Down Lonely Canyons

Fear corrodes my dreams tonight and mist has greyed
    my hills,
Mountains seem too tall to climb, December winds
    are chill.
There's no comfort on the earth, I am a child
    abandoned,
    Till I feel your hand in mine
    And laugh down lonely canyons.

Snow has bent the trees in grief, my summer dreams
    are dead,
Flowers are but ghostly stalks, the clouds drift
    dull as lead.
There's no solace in the sky, I am a child abandoned,
    Till we chase the dancing moon
    And laugh down lonely canyons.

Birds have all gone south too soon and frogs refuse to
    sing,
Deer lie hidden in the woods, the trout asleep till
    spring.
There's no wisdom in the wind, I am a child
    abandoned,
    Till we race across the fields
    And laugh down lonely canyons.

Darkness comes too soon tonight, the trees are silent
    scars,
Rivers rage against the rocks and snow conceals the
    stars.
There's no music in the air, I am a child abandoned,
    Till I feel my hand in yours
    And laugh down lonely canyons.

Wandering The Back Roads

Wandering the back roads
    Where peace greets me at dawn,
    And love and joy are waiting
        In gentleness at twilight
In the stillness of friendly hills and tranquil valleys.

Abandoning the highways
    Where the din of traffic stifles dreams
    And hurry and sadness abandon me
        To sameness and despair
Along the frenzied boulevards speeding nowhere.

Wandering the back roads
    Where I am reborn in serenity and laughter,
    Where a frightened child grown listless,
        Now rebounds in renewed energy and
The passionate ecstasy of a free and creative life.

Abandoning the highways
    Where the nameless, lonely ones
    Are lost in a faceless, winter fog
        That leads finally to the desolate cities
Of empty excitement and premature death.

Now life is my friend
    Whispering secrets never shared before,
    Transforming time into the ease of forever,
Where I see beauty privately fashioned,
    Hear music spontaneously composed
And smile helplessly—wandering the back roads.

Of Loneliness

Loneliness has taken its toll as I feared
    that I might miss some freedom
        in my commitment to you.
Loneliness kills the heart and dries the soul
    and focuses energy
On the narrow precipice of survival.
It passes only to return
    when the excitement vanishes
And I am again alone locked in the narrowness of
    my own heart.
Love expands, explodes, liberates,
    and is the final and only antidote to fear.
Loneliness kills the light and severs the connection
    with my world,
And only in reaching out to others
    does it seem to vanish.
We were made to love, to laugh,
    to rejoice in the day and night,
To lie together locked in security and comfort,
And to open our hearts to all who need us.
Now I only long for serenity and peace
    and to know that I am capable of love,
To listen and to hear, to give and receive,
    and each day to find the increasing energy
        that eluded me in pursuit of myself.

Time To Start Anew

Life has its beginnings
Coming at intervals,
Time to start anew.
None is first or last,
Save birth and death,
Nor can we decide
Which is most significant,
Transforming, or long enduring.
It only matters that
Each beginning, like spring,
Be given its due,
    To nourish the earth
        for flowers,
    To respect sun and rain
        for fertility
    Not to trample feeble life,
        our own or another's,
Before it is strong enough
    To bend in the wind!

Grateful

Grateful tonight for the sight
   of a single star,
Grateful for memories
   salvaged from afar.
Grateful for this time of silent peace,
Grateful beyond all words
   when the mad echoes cease.
Grateful for deliverance
   from a private hell,
Grateful beyond
   what a human voice can tell.
Grateful for the wonder of human love,
Grateful for some strange guidance
   from above.
Grateful for life,
   Grateful for rebirth,
     Grateful forever
   To live joyously on the earth.

Sometimes I Realize

Sometimes I realize
    That there are bus drivers who like their jobs
    Black kids who are happy
    Women who enjoy being mothers
    Freeway snarls that give people time to think
    Policemen who can make mistakes and laugh
    Old folks who aren't despondent
    Factory workers who hum all day
    Married couples who are in love
    Girls who aren't afraid to walk at night
    Kids who think school is really fun.
Sometimes I realize
    That there are teachers who enjoy their classes
    Longshoremen who think they're well paid
    Hunters who don't have a masculine hangup
    Children who love their parents
    Rich people who could be poor with dignity
    Girls who don't want bigger breasts
    Men and women who aren't afraid to die
    Doctors who care and don't overcharge
    Politicians who tell the truth.
Sometimes I realize that I am very happy.

New Language

I'm working on a new language, called
    Simplicity And Wonder.
It takes a while to learn it and demands
    a special lens for the eyes,
A hearing device created to catch sounds
    formerly unheard,
And currently I'm working on the new dictionary.
We've expunged "should", "ought", and "have to",
    "can't", "sin", "quilt", and "hell".
I wanted to leave out "peas", "okra", and "liver",
    but the board considered this personal bias.
We did get rid of "blame", "judgment", and "shame",
    but we managed to keep "moonshine" and "corn pone".
"Cholesterol" passed by a slim margin, but "diet"
    and "sacrifice" were extracted unanimously.
Some words will be permanently capitalized, like
    "PEACE", "SILENCE", "PLAY", and "MELLOW".
It took a lot of PLAY to get rid of "work",
    "stupid", "tragic", "superior", and "inferior".
There are some new words like "zipidoo" and "hopaloo",
    which are new ways of saying everything's MELLOW.
The new lenses reveal the heart of trees and flowers,
    the messages of stars and the shapes of clouds.
A hearing device catches the last words of dying leaves,
    the language of squirrels and the song of the wind.
Tomorrow we vote on getting rid of "gloom" and "despair",
    "hate", "revenge", "war", "satan", "greed",
        and "spinach".
Just get in touch and we'll keep you posted.
    Zipidoo!

Critical Voices

Critical voices rasping their religious wrath,
As if the appointed custodians and judges of history.
Now I no longer listen, my mind is fenced with
    "No Trespassing" signs,
And only the gentle and kind of heart are admitted.
Once I would have borne the pungent, scarring words
    of the self appointed elect
Like the confused and helpless child I was.
Now I guard that child with newly developed sinews
    of my own spiritual being,
Recreated in freedom by God Who watched over me
    from the beginning,
Who finally convinced me that the child within
    was fashioned in His very image.
And the man I am becoming,
    After a thousand essential detours and delays,
    Ten thousand abandoned fears and private victories,
Is ready to be what God had in mind at my creation.
And the critical voices rasping their religious wrath
Now have power to judge no one but themselves.

Becky's God

Becky's God is all thunderbolts and lightening sticks
    Ready to zap sinners with cancer and rivers
    of molten lava,
Not missing a single adulteress or roving husband,
    Keeping books on all of us like a compulsive accountant.
Becky's God thunders on Sinai and forbids Moses
      the promised land,
    Robs Job of herds and flocks and enthrones him
      on a dunghill,
    Opens the earth to swallow pagans and murders
      the eldest sons of Egypt,
    Decimates the folks in Jericho and introduces
      Samson to Delilah.

Becky's God killed Koreans and set fire to the villages
      of Vietnam,
    Murdered the Kennedy's and snuffed the temptress
      Marilyn Monroe,
    Cursed the Jews who killed His son, invented AIDS
      to wipe out homo's,
    Made blacks to serve the whites and shopping malls
      for sinners.

Come to think of it, Becky's God seems a lot like Becky!

Of Values

I learned about life
  From a child I hurt,
    From a woman I loved and made sad.
I learned about life
  From a feeble man's steps,
    From a friend I once thought I had.
I learned about life
  From a little boy's smile,
    From a woman's devotion to me.
I learned about life
  From a brave man I knew,
    From a friend who let me be free.
I learned about life
  From the first light of dawn,
    From the tales of a sycamore tree.
I learned about life
  From an owl at night
    From the earth sharing secrets with me.
I just couldn't learn
  From other men's Christs
    Or a memory of Moses in stone.
I learned about life
  By paying its price,
    By trying to stand up alone!

Sweet Anger

There's a sweet anger that lisps in meditation,
    Screams sinners to sudden conversion,
    Or speaks blithely of Buddhas and private gurus,
It often seems to me more vicious and insidious
    than the man or woman
Who spits anger out in honest fury and lets it go
    along the way.

Maybe God is only captured by those
    who know His archaic combination,
And "Om" or scream or bathe their way to intimacy
    and denied those who find Him on a golf course.
But one thing I do know, the pharisees were among
    the most avid prayer mongers, and
The man from Nazareth had some choice words for them.
He never made it complicated - a Father, a Son,
    a request, a faith, an answer.
It seems some who pray real well judge those who don't
And see the world as a weak and sickly place
    With all its sinners far below the heavens.
Thus anger, like vanity, hides itself in a thousand ways --
    sweetly, prayerfully, and judgmentally.
Fortunately God remains a Father to all His children,
    Even the lowliest and most unkempt.

Trusting

Trusting the day turning into moonlight,
Trusting snow drifts transformed into meadows,
Trusting the geese will return, and wheat and water
    will not disappear from the earth.
Trusting that children will laugh every morning
And hungry babies will cry for their mothers.
Trusting deer will survive the winter and mountains
    will forever guard the valleys.
Trusting most of all that sadness will pass and darkness
    will forever give way to dawn,
Trusting the love locked in my heart and the light
    locked in my eyes
Will shine on every step I take, every voice I hear,
    every face I finally see.
Trusting you, trusting me, trusting life, trusting God!

To Walk

To walk when you fear to keep going,
To stand when you long to lie down,
To believe when there's no way of knowing,
To seek when there's naught to be found,
To live with regrets without bending,
To love without hope of return,
To begin when you don't know the ending,
To give a hundred times more than you earn.
To smile when you doubt about living,
To laugh when you'd like to despair,
To forgive when you're filled with misgiving,
To survive when none seems to care.
To try when success is a stranger,
To persist when strength disappears,
To confront the threatening dangers,
To challenge a lifetime of fears.
To look till you find what you're after,
To search earth and the vastness above,
To trust in the power of laughter,
And the final victory of love.

I Want To Die A Careless Man

I want to die a careless man
    With my yellow legal pages scattered on the floor,
My desk covered with ashes and unfinished thoughts,
    Borne away on the wind of an idea,
    Not far from one who loves me
        And understands enough of my madness
        To stay until the end.
I have not learned much of life,
Each evening a new mystery to wonder about,
    Struggling somehow to stay alive
    Among so many satisfied to survive.
Tonight I have no time for prophets or profit margins,
    I do not worry about the failure of socialism,
    Or the vandalism on buses after school.
    Nor do I care what the President thinks.
I would like to watch a flock of ducks
    Circle a swamp three times before landing,
    Eavesdrop on coyotes at the edge of a forest,
    And hear church bells across a quiet valley.
Most of all I would like to die a careless man.

Grey Whales

The grey whales screaming plaintively into the night,
  Weeping, laughing, moaning, loving,
Begging a mate to hear their pain and longing,
Begging a whole world to understand
  Their journey from Arctic shores, their flight
    from human enemies,
Recalling their ancient courage and drawn to
  secret lagoons,
Memories borrowed from long before the birth of man,
And hoping that a tender heart will finally hear
  And shatter the loneliness of their long excursion.
As predictable as waves and the tides that guide them.

Somehow I share their profound memory, as if an angel
  directs me from the primal light of creation,
As I now make my way through each year of my life,
  Weeping, laughing, moaning, loving,
And hope that I will finally be led to a safe harbor of
  intimacy and joy,
That my pulsing, silent screams will be heard,
And I will make the endless journey
  In a deep abiding love,
In eternal union with the whales.

It's Time To Start Again

It's time to start again,
    Forget mistakes I've made
    And wounds inflicted
        By those who vowed to love me.
It's scary looking back
    At all the missed opportunities,
    The wrong roads,
    Hesitations that should have been decisions,
    Impulses that should have been slept on—for
        months.
Somehow I was infallible,
    My own Vatican,
    Sure of everything,
    Afraid of nothing,
    Confident that all would be as it ever was,
    Content with my collected platitudes when I
        wasn't hearing.
So much arrogance, so much ignorance,
    So much ingratitude, so much fury,
    So much struggling to get somewhere
        That I could ignore those who loved me.
A man rushing in every direction,
    Certain that some frantic move would bare life's
        secret,
        Or canonize him forever.

Now it's time to start again—slowly, cautiously,
     Like a child examining the world for the very
          first time,
Tired of seeing life at 32,000 feet or even 32,
     Tired of seeing human pain and simple joy as
          mere color patterns on a mad journey
          to nowhere.
It's time to start again,
     Quietly, lovingly, gratefully,
With time left over I never knew I had,
     Time to see and hear
To be grateful, and finally,
     To love.

One Day

One day, when stars had disappeared and
 mountains were no longer my friends,
When my favorite river was grey and insensitive
 even to spring's bursting melodies and the
 eloquent Nevada sky said nothing,
When I had lost interest in birds and even trees,
 and the moon upon the giant lake was pale
 and disinterested in earth,
When life had lost flavor and death
 was an unknown terror,
 I was buried in the muck of
 my own despairing.
All former joys were silent, friends had disappeared,
 hope seemed pointless and a dispassionate God
 ignored my imploring,
And there was no one to turn to
 save the poverty I had become,
When my heart begged to break and my eyes
 were glazed with crusty tears
 and I could endure the pain no longer,
I fell upon the ground unable to walk or even crawl,
 admitting life had won and I was alone
 attempting to stand upright on the earth,
That no one could understand the terror
 and loss of confidence I felt,
When love and sex and even gentle touching
 were denied me, and all the gifts I once used
 so facilely were transformed to ineloquent
 stone and stubbornly refused me,

When there was no apparent reason to live
    except I feared the emptiness of death,
I knew that a single yearning appetite could rouse me
    to the beginning of some personal,
        remote salvation,
A single passion, though feeble, could provide
    the light and energy of reconciliation with myself.
And from deep within some cavern of my soul
    heretofore unexplored,
A single word erupted and echoed like a pebble
    rolling down a mountain and said:
"Endure! Endure! The rhythm will return in its
    own time if you do not violate
        some code of honesty with yourself.
"Flowers will reappear, music will return
    to restore your soul!"
Thus slowly I rose from the bottom of the pit
    when every fibre of my being screamed
        for me to lie there still.
I rose up, only to endure, and in the morning
    —for an instant—again saw the sun,
        and rejoiced for the briefest moment
            that I was still alive.
It was then I knew that I would indeed endure,
    and the ever-present pain of some purging
        would finally disappear,
And joy would be forever mine
    in my lonely and redemptive enduring!

Today

Today I stand like God astride the sky and chaos,
   Creating my own world in seven days or
      seven centuries,
Bringing the sun into focus, and celebrating
   The golden aspen trees and blushing peonies
      That fall from my fingertips,
   Gathering swans and fawns from the dust,
   Building orange mountains at twilight,
      And carving out peaceful valleys.
   Boldly I bid the splashing, silver rivers
      To fill the ocean
      And set in motion the repetitious waves.
   Each tulip and crocus is my own creation,
   Each wooded path and creeping vine is my invention.
At the end of the final day, I lovingly create myself,
      And fashion from the rib
      That guards my heart, a bride.
Only then, like God, I rest!

Beyond A Misty Hill

Some people never go there,
  Perhaps they never will.
There's an unmarked road
To a silent grove
  Beyond a misty hill.
They don't send invitations,
  I doubt they ever will.
You walk alone
To a place I've known
  Beyond a misty hill.
Most will never find it,
  For life's a daily drill,
But the ones like me
Find a kind of peace
  Beyond a misty hill.
There are no maps describing,
  It can't be found by skill.
It's an unmarked road
To a silent grove
  Beyond a misty hill.
It's an unmarked road to a silent grove
  Beyond a misty hill.

Life Has Its Beginnings

Life has its beginnings,
    Each with its own
Special promises,
    Each a door opening
To some new wonder,

Each a unique melody fashioned
    in our hearts,
Each a personal adventure
    even as at time's beginning
When darkness was dispelled
    and the sun and moon
Were first appointed to guard
    the heavens and lovingly
To guide the day and night.

Such beginnings are a renewal
    of our very being,
A sometimes fragile gift
    That must be tended and loved,
    Nourished and understood,
Until all that can be, will be,
And life continues to be
    a joyful creation
Of promises and original melodies
    and endless new beginnings.

Clouds

Letting life happen as it will,
Like a directionless cloud that moves in majesty,
  And thus finally with wisdom.
Passing through other clouds and even mountains
  Without anger.
Drawing water without greed, and showering the earth
  Without pride of hostility.
Simply a cloud floating wherever it must float.
Grown graceful in every wind, and darkened
  Without losing grace,
Rising and falling as is destined,
Content with the sky's gift of space
  With no thought of replacing the sun,
And gratefully enlightened by the moon.
  Friend of the earth and everyone,
A dancing, smiling, silent, balloon
  Without protest or pretense,
Without ambition or lost innocence,
Letting life happen as it will.

Some Were Sent

Some were sent to gather lonely people
    shadows hiding in the night,
Stone-facedly ignoring sunshine,
    Lost in emptiness and flight,
Still afraid of soft surrender
    The things they can't possess.
Marching in a somber procession
    Where none is cursed or blest,
Those bereft of love or caring
    In silences that never end,
Where voices echo loneliness
    And souls refuse to mend.

Some were sent to gather lonely people,
    Their pain a license to understand,
Their odyssey's tenacious living,
    Clinging to a feeble patch of land,
Girded with a softened heart,
    Warmed with time and tears,
Burning with undying flames,
    Wounded monarchs of their fears,
Grateful for the privilege
    To teach limping knights to fight,
To summon all the lonely people
    From the darkness of their fright.

Love is their only weapon,
    Patience their only skill,
Wisdom garnered from their knowing,
    Only desperation kills.

To Let Go

I long to let go, to release all the illusions
    That separate me from what is,
To feel my body pulse and soar, lifting my mind from
    its timidity and repairing all the ancient
    scars of my soul,
To float through the day and dance into the night,
    Following the directions of winds and clouds
    and ever in touch with the earth.
To feel my roots descend into the deep waters of the
    earth's core like a palm tree in the desert,
    strong because it bends,
Unafraid because it flows with water and life.
I am not the solid, unshaken oak, I am leaves flying
    from branches,
    Scattered and helpless on the ground.
I am an evergreen, not high on a mountain, but
    nestled in a valley by a stream, playing
    with children
      Flying kites from my branches, loving the birds
        that rest there,
    Laughing in the sunshine and weeping softly in
      the rain,
Letting go of all I ever aspired to be,
    For I am already loved, and that alone is
      beyond all illusion.

To Begin To Live The Rest Of My Life

It makes no sense to my friends back home
That a middle-aged man should want to roam.
But I left the money and a share of fame
And I called it quits in the business game;
I left a house and a proper wife,
    To begin to live the rest of my life.

It makes no sense to my swinging friends
That a middle-aged man should begin again.
So the stories grew and the rumors rolled
As the tale of my madness was oft retold.
But I can bear the gossip's knife
    To begin to live the rest of my life.

It makes no sense to society
That a middle-aged man would take his leave.
The briefcase boys just shook their head,
My mother said I was better off dead.
But I packed my bag without advice
    To begin to live the rest of my life.

It makes no sense to my neighborhood
That a middle-aged man is gone for good.
The preacher bowed his head and prayed,
My father said I should have stayed,
But I went away with the rumors rife
    To begin to live the rest of my life.

Well I'm lonely now but my heart is free,
I enjoy a beer and watch a tree,
I can see a cloud and feel the breeze,
I can buy some bread and a bit of cheese.
And I know full well it is my right
      To begin to live the rest of my life.

Now I have no plans for security,
No proper wife can depend on me,
I'm not too sure of eternity
But I know when a heart is really free.
And I walk along with a step that's light
      To begin to live the rest of my life.

Love And Breath Beyond Belief

Love and life and breath beyond belief
And dreams all destined to be fulfilled,
   A heart too full to make sense,
   With giraffes dancing with kangaroos
   And songs lustier than a pumpkin moon,
   With dancing stars and every moment making love
   And bearing children too winsome to weep,
   A hand long enough to reach the heavens
   And to tickle them until they can only giggle
   And shout delightedly:
"My God, it's beautiful! It's man!"

Dawn Comes

Dawn comes without warning
   To tell of life again and morning unexpected.
It is always a surprise, life I mean,
Never what I anticipate, and seldom what I ask.
I have wanted a thousand things
   Enough money to sail the seas forever
   Enough friends never to know loneliness
   Enough sex languorously given in sunlight.
Now I only ask
   That a tree smile at me
   The sky never hide its face again
   The song of a bird heard in reverence
   And a gentle lover who knows
      each mounting fear
      each budding joy.
No longer can I attack life. It is the master,
   No matter what the unscarred young heroes say.
I am but leaves and wind, clouds and rain,
   Sun and sand and iris at the edge of the garden.
I am lilac trees and cherry blossoms,
   Lilies of the valley and violet paths in forests.
No more, no less.
   My heart sings when it sings
   Weeps when it weeps
   And loves when it can
As dawn comes — without warning.

At Times

At times the mountains seem insurmountable now
As I gaze at them from the safety of a warm,
    flowering meadow
There is snow upon the peaks and chill winds
    gust angrily above me.
Yet, as beautiful as the meadow is, I have been
    here too long
And the song of birds has grown dull,
The flowers seem artificial, and the frogs
    too content.
I want to fly myself above the peaks, sing
    my own songs,
And climb till every vestige of every dream
    is silent.
Why am I afraid to travel where destiny draws me?
Why do I hesitate when a familiar echo deep
    in the caverns of my heart calls me?
This is no time to reminisce, to watch
    the circling crows and drifting clouds.
It is time to move lest winter harden my limbs
    and freeze my fantasies.
It is time to move boldly and bravely and remember
That the purest air is waiting in the heights
And a single step is enough to be on my way!

Hurrying Through Life

Hurrying through life like a child
    Forever anticipating some joy tomorrow,
    Afraid to miss something
And missing damn near everything!
    Afraid to build a dream step by step
And to wait for all that is destined.
    Ready to take the instant pleasure lest we die
And missing all the simple beauty
    Of planting in the spring
    Harvesting in the summer
And of wondering and loving and dreaming all year long
Who will teach us to walk slowly
    To grasp each moment
And to understand
    That what now is
Will never be again.

Of The Arctic

I am as cold tonight
    As the dull darkness of the Arctic,
    As whales snorting and playing their way
        south in frigid waters,
    As the silent, glacier mountain reflecting
        a lost and lonely heart,
    As a wandering, frightened child making his way
        across the ice.
I am the Arctic tonight, the whale, the lonely heart,
    The child who hears but his own echo
        in the frigid solitude.
I have lost my way, gambled away the sun's heat,
    Ignored even the feeble warmth of stars,
Screamed to snowdrifts and bitter, laughing winds, finally
    Aware that no one listens to my plaintive sounds.
I walk above snow covered fences and inch my way
        along buried roads,
    Guard my chafed and frozen face helplessly against
        the cold,
    Feel numbed feet grow thick and motionless within
        my boots.
Only you bring me warmth, but you are far away,
    Warmed by another sun,
    Sheltered by the fire of an unfamiliar hearth.
Life floats by like my frozen breath, and I wonder about
    Decisions I have made and battles I have lost,
Even as the night grows colder
In the dull darkness of the Arctic.

Yet, tomorrow the sun will rise and reappear,
   And freshly fallen snow will sparkle like diamonds
      in its guiding light,
And a lost child, like the snorting, playful whales,
   Will make his way to the warm and silent
      place inside my heart,
Where the sun will rise and set upon command,
   ice will melt,
   And the glaciers will prism all my favorite colors
      in the light within!

The Sun Lingers

The sun lingers over the ocean a little longer tonight,
While I remember everyone I love
    And wish I could hold them in my arms
    all at once.
Words are so futile to speak of love, to heal hurts so
    pointless and unintended.
Perhaps life's greatest pain and longing is the
    loneliness of missing friends I cannot call
    to my side.
Curse time and distance and all the banalities of life
    that tear us apart!
I didn't know when I left home I would leave the
    brothers I loved.
Time was so omnipresent, we had every day, every
    meal, forever.
I wish as I watch the disappearing sun that I could
    gather together all those I love and all
    that love me,
And remain in one house, one town, one union.
No one left out, no one unavailable, no one whose
    voice and words and smile could not be at my
    beck and call.
I miss you all so much,
    And love you all so profoundly,
And refuse to understand a world and destiny that
    keeps us apart.

But I am grateful for the friends that life has
    permitted to remain,
Grateful for the memories, the reunions that
    lie ahead,
    The laughs and tears and stories that cannot be
        told enough,
Grateful that the sun lingers over the ocean a little
    longer tonight.

Most Of All

Most of all
  I like the trees,
    Rooted in the earth,
    Silent and unafraid to be alone,
  Proud in a forest
  Or strong and solitary in a meadow,
Refusing to fall until the very end.
If I were to be born again,
  It would not be with Jesus
    Or his sacred rivals,
  Not with a grinning therapist
    Who has been shaped
      By what I have discarded.
I want to be born again with the trees
  Under sun and sky.
To wake up every morning
  And never wonder why.

Sadness Is But A Part Of It All

Sadness is but a part of it all
Coming so relentlessly in the morning,
The offscouring of dreams.
　Why do you run?
The birch tree does not run
Stripped of his leaves by the cold winds,
　Waiting silently all winter
　　Without complaint
　Standing knee deep in the snow
　　Without motion.
He knows the cold will go away
That the sun will warm the grass green
　And give back his leaves
　And lure back his birds.
He knows that only fools are not sad.

A Stone

Once a little stone
   Was lying in a field
Till someone picked him up
   Polished him
Joined him with other stones
   And made him part of a wall.
He wasn't a stone anymore
   Free to lie in the dust
Until the rain came
   To make him clean again.
He was cemented in a wall
   Surrounded, crowded by other stones.
He was hardly noticed before
   Now everyone saw the wall
Of which he was a part.
   But the wall was in a field
And did nothing, protected nothing
   Led to nothing.
It was only a wall in a field
   Standing alone made by men
Who thought they should use the stone for something.
   And the little stone will remain there
Till the wall falls down
   Or someone knocks it down.
Then he will be a stone again
   And get dusty, feel the rain
And the soft feet of children.

Peace

In a complex and oft confusing world,
When life's details
    Get in the way of living,
And mounting worries
Crowd out simple beauty
    Of snow and silence,
    Fresh water and flowers,
When tragedy strikes without warning
And suffering arrives unannounced,
Then most of all
    We must cling to what is truly beautiful--
    Children, love, laughter, dreams,
    Wisdom, wonder, all that friendship means,
Rearranging priorities, and taking time
    To discover what is alien,
    What is really mine.
'Tis then confusion softens, storms cease,
'Tis then descends the gift of private peace.
May such peace surround our lives
    And fill our space,
May peace transform our hearts
    And thus our race.

Finally

Finally I want so little of life,
Merely to let me run free,
To greet each day with some excitement and
    new found hope.
I ask not fame or fortune, but some quiet tranquility
    that lives within me at all times,
And does not fear loss or storm, life or death, or
    whatever is mine to confront.
I cannot recall the past or remake it, I cannot live
    with regrets of what I have or have not done.
I can only hold on to a Father's hand knowing His
    strength is mine.
Life is this moment, the lady walking the dog, cars
    parked by the side of the road,
Lovers holding hands briefly in the morning chill.

Fear is a strange and persistent enemy—I find it hard
    to fight him directly lest he overwhelm me.
I let him pass through my being and know that he has
    no more currency
Than strange sounds I heard in the basement as a child.
I've learned too much from fear to hide it under a bushel.
I've traveled too many roads finally to turn back,
    loved too much to be denied.
I no longer want the whole world, just my own gentle
    place of service and love,
And the courage and strength from God to do today
    and tomorrow whatever I was forever meant to do.

Information About Books, Tapes And Appearances By James Kavanaugh

In September 1990, all rights to James Kavanaugh books were purchased by Steven J Nash who is now the exclusive publisher of Kavanugh's books and tapes. For information, write:

STEVEN J. NASH PUBLISHING
P. O. Box 2115 Highland Park, IL 60035
or call: 1-708-433-6731

BOOKS BY JAMES KAVANAUGH

There Are Men Too Gentle To Live Among Wolves. The James Kavanaugh classic in its 67th printing! He writes: "I am one of the searchers... We searchers are ambitious only for life itself, for everything it can provide... we want to love and be loved, to live in a relationship that will not...prevent our search, nor lock us in prison walls..."

Will You Be My Friend? *(57th printing)* Kavanaugh writes: "Friendship is freedom, is flowing, is rare... It trusts, understands, grows, explores, it smiles and weeps. It does not exhaust or cling, expect or demand. It is— and that is enough—and it dreams a lot!"

Laughing Down Lonely Canyons. Kavanaugh confronts human loneliness and fear. He writes: "This is a book for the barely brave like me who refuse to abandon their dream... It is for those who want to make of life the joy it was meant to be, who refuse to give up no matter the pain..."

From Loneliness To Love. Kavanaugh writes: "To move from loneliness to love means to take a risk, to create the kind of personal environment and support we need. This is a book of hope and reassurance that love is available and loneliness can end."

Search: A Guide For Those Who Dare Ask Of Life Everything Good And Beautiful. *(Prose)* "**Search** provides 12 proven principles to move from self doubt through self awareness to self love. It is a celebration of one's creativity and unique beauty, rising from practical psychology to the spiritual power of our Inner Being in a journey to wholeness."

Today I Wondered About Love. *(formerly, Faces In The City)*. This book was written in San Francisco and captured the soul of that most human of cities. Herein are some of Kavanaugh's most profound and gently humorous reflections on the man-woman experience and the quest for personal freedom.

Maybe If I Loved You More. These passionate, lyrical poems confront forces that numb our senses and corrupt our values. Kavanaugh challenges us to be fully human, to move past private fears to simplicity and joy: "So much of life is spent trying to prove something...Maybe if I loved you more, I wouldn't have to prove anything!"

Sunshine Days And Foggy Nights. This work contains Kavanaugh's most tender love poems, like the wondrous *Fragile Woman*: "too tender for sex, who will surely die—if tonight I do not love you." He speaks of the energy of any creative life: "The work I find most significant drains the least energy...my distractions are usually more creative than my resolutions."

Winter Has Lasted Too Long. Kavanaugh sings of personal freedom and real love in a superb preface: "We shall be as free as we want, as mad as we are, as honest as we can. We shall accept no price for our integrity...This book is a heart's recognition that truth matters, love is attainable, and spring will begin tomorrow."

Walk Easy On The Earth. A book inspired by Kavanaugh's years spent in a remote cabin in the California gold country. "I do not focus on the world's despair, I am forever renewed by spring splashing over granite rocks, or a cautious deer emerging into twilight. I know then that I will survive all my personal fears and realize my finest dreams."

A Village Called Harmony-A Fable. A powerful, eloquent prose tale that touches the deepest chords in the human struggle of lust and love, passion and peace. Dear Abby says: "It is a powerful tale of our times. A classic! I loved it!"

Celebrate The Sun: A Love Story. A moving prose allegory about the life of Harry Langendorf Pelican, dedicated to "those who take time to celebrate the sun—and are grateful!" A stirring tale that touches the very core of love—loving oneself.

The Crooked Angel. James Kavanaugh's only children's story tells of two angels "with crooked little wings" who escape from isolation and sadness through friendship and laughter... A particular Christmas delight. Says Goldie Hawn: "My children loved it! So did I."

Tears And Laughter Of A Man's Soul. James Kavanaugh writes: "Men are not easy to know, even by other men...It's a rare woman who understands men...we hope another marriage, a secret affair, or more income will revive us...ingrained habits only assume a new addictive form, depression fills a vacuum of dead dreams...the path to freedom and joy is more exciting than difficult."

Quiet Water: The Inspirational Poems Of James Kavanaugh. In this powerful new edition of his own favorites, Kavanaugh gives hope and courage when life's most difficult passages seem impossible to endure. He writes with the wisdom and compassion born of his own painful discovery of the path to peace and joy. A perfect gift for a struggling friend!..."There is quiet water in the center of your soul..."

Mystic Fire: The Love Poems Of James Kavanaugh. All the passion, romance, and tenderness, as well as the humor and pain of love unfold in this beautiful new edition of Kavanaugh's favorite love poems. Men and women of any age, will find herein the perfect gift, on any occasion, celebrating the expression of love... "Love grew like some mystic fire around my heart..."

In addition to his books Kavanaugh also has a selection of poetry readings and lectures on audio/video tape available through Steven J. Nash Publishing.

About the author

James Kavanaugh exploded onto the American scene in 1967 with **A Modern Priest Looks At His Outdated Church.** The New York Times called it "a personal cry of anguish that goes to the heart of the troubles plaguing the Catholic Church. "Though a gifted scholar, with degrees in psychology and religious philosophy, he surrendered his priestly collar and doctoral robes to become a "gentle revolutionary".

Twenty years ago in a decrepit New York residence hotel, Kavanaugh rejected lucrative offers to write what publishers wanted. "Feasting", he laughs, "on bagels, peanut butter, and cheese whiz", he wrote his first poetry book, **There Are Men Too Gentle To Live Among Wolves.** The book was turned down by a dozen publishers, only to sell over a million copies.

Wayne Dyer captures his power:

"James Kavanaugh is America's poet laureate. His words and ideas touch my soul. I can think of no living person who can put into words what we have all felt so deeply in our inner selves."

A dozen poetry books followed, as well as powerful novels, prose allegory, and his best-selling **Search**, a guide for personal joy and freedom. The rebel priest became the people's poet, singing songs of human struggle, of hope and laughter, of healing that comes from within.

James Kavanaugh possesses a charisma that excites audiences with passion and humor. He loves wandering, tennis and trout fishing, the cities and wilderness, people and solitude.